EMBROIDERY BUSINESS FROM HOME

Business model and digitizing training course

by Martin Barnes

Volume 1: Business Model

This publication is designed to provide accurate and authoritative information with regard to the subject matter covered. It is sold with the understanding that the publisher and the author are not engaged in rendering legal, accounting, or other professional advice. If legal advice or other expert assistance is required, the services of a competent professional person should be sought.

Copyright © 2016 www.embroideryhomebusiness.com, Martin Barnes
All rights reserved.
This book, or parts thereof, may not be reproduced in any form without permission from the author. For more information you can contact us at
info@embroideryhomebusiness.com

Table of Contents

Chapter 1 - Basic things to know about Embroidery 5
   What is embroidery 5
   Modern embroidery 6
   The size of the embroidery industry 6
   How to make a living out of embroidery 7
   What you need to invest in – Estimated cost 8
   Embroidery digitizing 10

Chapter 2 - Embroidery Machines 12
   Types of machines 12
   Types of connections with the Computer 20
   Machines for home based business 22
   List of machine brands 26
   How to choose the best machine for you 32
   Outsourcing embroidery 33

Chapter 3 – Embroidery Digitizing 38
   What is Embroidery Digitizing 38
   List of embroidery software developers 39
   How to choose the best embroidery software for you 43
   Embroidery files 46

Chapter 4 – The business model of home based embroidery 50
   Where to start from 50
   Niche market 52
   Overview of the business model 53
      Your website 53
      How the business works 55
      Where to advertise 56
      Additional Income 60
      Initial Investment Analysis 61
   Sum up 63

How to get the Free Embroidery Designs 65

Pictures, charts, tables and images.

Pictures

Picture 1 – Multi – head machine in an embroidery unit in Mumbai 5
Picture 2 – Tajima Single-head Multi-needle Embroidery Machine 13
Picture 3 – Different Hoops Sizes 15
Picture 4 – Barudan 20 Head Embroidery Machine 16
Picture 5 – Singer Single-head Single-needle Embroidery Machine 17
Picture 6 – DB 25 Serial Cable 21
Picture 7 – Logos to digitize with starter software 46

Charts

Chart 1 – Decorated Apparel Industry size 7
Chart 2 – Production per Month and Cost of Embroidery Machine 23

Tables

Table 1 - Comparison of Single-needle and Multi-needle Machines 20
Table 2 – Embroidery File-types 49
Table 3 – Initial Investment required 62

Images

Image 1 - Typical embroidery software screen 9

Chapter 1 - Basic things to know about Embroidery

What is embroidery

Embroidery is the craft of decorating fabrics or other materials with needle and thread or yarn. In many cases embroidery may also incorporate other materials as well, like pearls, beads, sequins etc.

Handmade embroidery goes back to the 5th century BC, and continued to work with similar techniques for many centuries. Industrial embroidery came in stages from 1800 until our days, but some 40 years ago a revolution took place, and machine embroidery changed the industry upside down. In 1977, Barudan, one of the biggest Japanese embroidery machine manufacturers, created the first multi – head embroidery machine (see picture 1). Mass production changed the world as we knew it up to then, and big firms exploited the opportunity which stood in front of them, in order to make big profit.

Picture 1 – Multi – head machine in an embroidery unit in Mumbai

In our days though, the face of the industry seems to be changing again. Mass production firms are going bankrupt, and production is moving to lower cost countries like China. Some think that there's nothing to be done about it. Others, the clever ones, are preparing to make a lot of money out of the new trend that is here to stay for many years to come. Its name is "personalization", and I'm going to teach you how to make money out of it from your home.

Modern embroidery

Modern embroidery has nothing to do with old handmade embroidery. Most contemporary embroidery is being done using computerized embroidery machines. A person called "digitizer" or "puncher" uses specialized software called "embroidery software", in order to transform an image, for example a logo, into embroidery. Then this design file, which is called "embroidery design", is transferred to the embroidery machine in order to embroider it onto the desired material, e.g. fabric. It sounds difficult, but with proper training, it is possible today for one person to handle both the digitizing and the embroidery process. In other words, today's technology allows a person to handle the production of a finished embroidery product by himself. Moreover, in today's globalized market, it's not the quantity that brings the real profit, it's the quality. That is mainly the quality of digitizing, and secondly the quality of embroidery. If the digitizer does a crappy work, then whatever the embroiderer does, and however good work he does, the end result cannot be better than the actual digitizing quality. So, digitizing is the first step, and in my opinion the most important one in modern embroidery. That is why there are many embroiderers, but few digitizers. When you finish this course, you will be able to create a state of the art embroidery design, and consider yourself a quality digitizer.

The size of the embroidery industry

Decorated apparel is a $14 billion industry which is estimated to grow to $20 billion at the end of the second decade of the 21st century. The previous decade was an $8 billion industry and the decade before that a $4 billion. The industry seems to double itself each decade. It is predicted that its growth will continue for many decades to come.

The decorated apparel industry includes screen printers and embroiderers. The embroidery Indus-try is estimated to be approximately one third of the decorated apparel industry. That means we are talking about a $4.6 billion industry today, which will become $6.6 billion industry in 5-10 years.

Now, you must ask yourself why this industry has such a big growth rate which seems unstoppable. The magic word is "personalization". People just love personalized products more and more as years pass by. People want to be able to order a

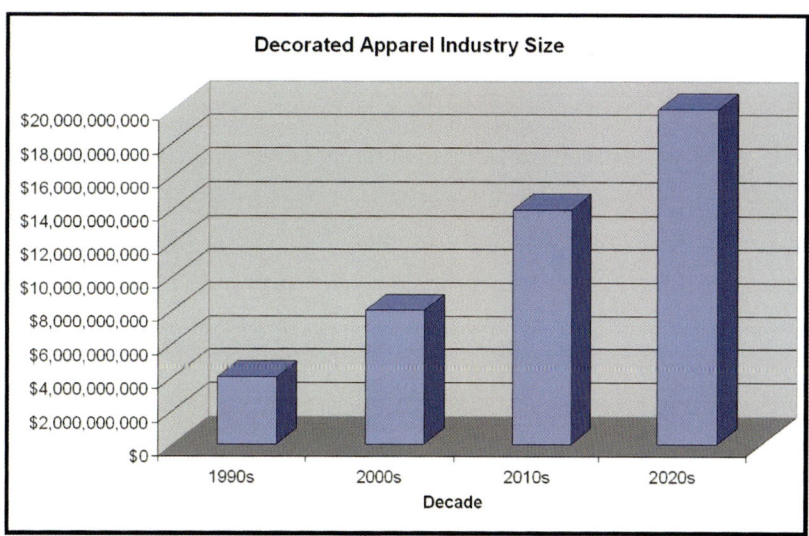

Chart 1 – Decorated Apparel Industry size

shirt with their name on it, or with an image they love. Small companies, the spine of modern western economies, want their logos embroidered on shirts or towels or hats. This trend is growing more and more, and big industries cannot offer this, because simply it's not profitable for them to produce such low quantities. Small enterprises started filling the gap, and making substantial profit out of it. My estimate is that whoever comes in the next five to seven years can have a very good ROI. After that I believe there are maybe another 5 years of reasonable ROI, and after that the competition will be fierce. But the important thing is that NOW is the time to enter. Whoever tries it will surely have good profit with very low investment amount for starting.

How to make a living out of embroidery

So, how does one make a living out of embroidery from home? Well, first of all one needs to understand what he needs to do, and if he is able to do it. It's not simple, it's not easy, but it's not rocket science. With proper training anyone can do it. With this course you will have all the information you will need in order to evaluate if you want to do this, and also all the tools and training, not only to get you started, but also to be on a higher level of education. The photos in the books and the training videos that are included in this course will make you familiar with both software and hardware that you will need to use, in order to operate your business. The study material and examples will make you an advanced digitizer and embroiderer.

After one takes the decision to start this, he will have to start learning. There are a lot of things to learn before starting. You must first of all decide which hardware and software to buy and where from. The good news is that you don't have to do any research at all, since you will find detailed info on embroidery machines as well as embroidery software in this course. Lists of available embroidery machines with detailed features and indicative prices, including various types of machines, lists of embroidery software with detailed features and indicative prices from various developers, all packed inside this course for you. You will even find a guide which will help you decide how to choose your starting equipment, depending on your goals and your budget. So, don't worry about making mistakes on choosing the wrong hardware or software, or about how big your investment should be. Once you finish this course, you will be certain of exactly what you need to buy, and what amount you will have to spend for it.

Most importantly, I will share with you all the secrets of the industry; which company has a good name on the market, and which only has good marketing department with crappy products. You won't have to worry if you made a good purchase or not, and if the company will support you well or not. I will tell you what's on the market today. Only a very informed insider can give you this valuable info, and I will share it with you in this course.

In Chapter 3, you will even find the complete business model proposed for embroidery business from home, and exactly what you need to do in order to start making big bucks out of embroidery.

What you need to invest in – Estimated cost

Let's move on, and see what you will need to invest in order to start an embroidery business from home.

The first essential thing you need to invest in is embroidery machine. Depending on how big you need your business to be and what kind of work you need to focus on, you can choose from various types of embroidery machines. In Chapter 2, you will find a detailed description of different types of embroidery machines, and information on the usage of each one. The price range starts from $1,000 up to about $18,000 depending on the machine. In Chapter 2, when you will understand the differences in machine types, you will know which machine is best for you. The price varies depending on the type and the brand of the machine. "Big brand" machines are more expensive, while "smaller brands" as well as Chinese made machines are of lower price. Also, this price range does not include multi – head machines, because these are not appropriate at least for the initial stages of the business this course is all about, that is work from home. For your information though, there are multi – head machines with various head numbers, from 2 up to 56. A machine like this might start at $30.000 and go very high in price. Of course second hand machines are always a choice when it comes to multi – head, even single-head embroidery machines.

You will find all detailed info about prices in Chapter 3 "The business model of home based embroidery".

The second essential thing you need to invest in is embroidery software. There are many embroidery software developers in the world. Some sell complete products, while others sell products in different levels, or add-ons to a basic level. I will guide you through this very difficult decision. Marketing plays a very important role in this field as well, by manipulating people in buying low quality products in high prices. I will provide detailed information on the biggest companies in the world

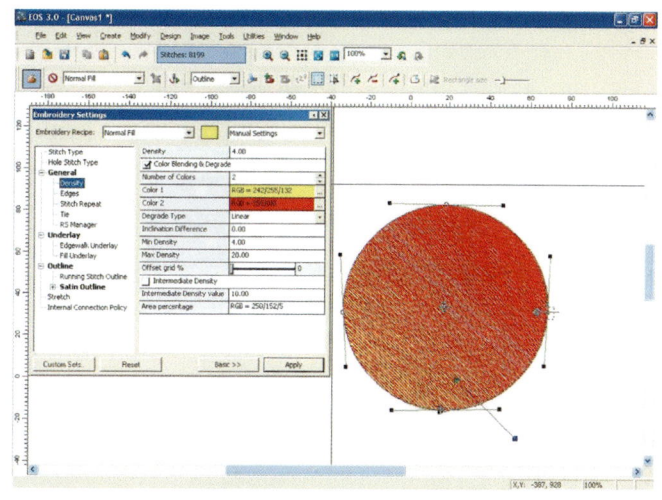

Image 1 - Typical embroidery software screen

that offer quality software, because as I said, the process of embroidery digitizing is the most important of all in the embroidery business chain. The cost of embroidery software might start at around $300 for lower level software and can go up to several thousands of dollars. Probably a cost of $1000 is realistic for a starter, with the ability to upgrade in the future when his will need to expand. In Chapter 3, you will find a list of embroidery software developers, and detailed information on their products. Of course inside information will be shared with you about this as well.

The third essential thing you need to invest in, is a website and advertising. Today's world runs through the internet. Commerce has changed, production is adapting, and the smart ones are already making millions of dollars out of the internet. I will get you online, tell you the secrets of an online presence and how you can make your embroidery business number one on your field by focusing on niche markets.

In Chapter 3 you will find all appropriate info.

Embroidery digitizing

Embroidery digitizing is the process where artwork is converted into digital data, which is then used to get it stitched onto a piece of fabric or other material through a computerized embroidery machine.

As we have already pinpointed, embroidery digitizing is a very important part of the embroidery business, probably the most important one. If embroidery is badly digitized, there is nothing you can do in order to counterbalance this flaw with careful embroidery on the embroidery machine. So, the actual embroidery design must be perfect, and good finished embroidery outcome, starts with a perfect design. The actual embroidery on the machine has it challenges as well, but this can be overcome with trial and error, since this is the last part of the embroidery process.

Now, another thing you might want to have in mind is that embroidery digitizing is expensive, and there are not many digitizers that offer good services at a low price, if any. All low priced digitizing services on the internet today are of very low quality. So, by learning how to digitize yourself, you will have two major advantages. You will be able to create flawless embroidery designs for you, which, as we saw, is a very important link of the embroidery chain, plus you will be able to offer your digitizing services to others, a business that is very well paid in our days for good digitizers.

In Chapter 3 we will examine all possibilities for your new business, including some outsourcing options.

Because digitizing is the most important part of the embroidery process, in BOOK 2, plus all the extra material of this course, I will teach you how to digitize perfect quality designs, which you can embroider on various materials, or sell them to others. I will share digitizing secrets only high quality digitizers know, and of course do not share with people outside the industry.

Chapter 2 - Embroidery Machines

According to statistics, before 1997 there were only a few factories specialized in computer embroidery machine making with a total production of no more than 2000 sets or so annually. After 1998, both the number of embroidery machine manufacturers and their volume doubled. In 2004 the total number of manufacturing factories increased to more than 150, specialized parts suppliers totaled more than 2000 companies with yearly turnover more than 40,000 sets. The industry is thriving and today's expansion is even bigger. Inevitably, China and other low cost countries entered the machine manufacturing industry, and the competition is even fiercer. The result was that recently, embroidery machine prices dropped significantly. The last obstacle for people who wanted to enter the embroidery industry was lifted, and the wise businessmen started exploiting this opportunity the smart way. They are not focusing in mass production any more, while the ones that do are doomed to bankrupt if they haven't already. Today is the best time than ever to start an embroidery business from home.

Now, let's start with the basics concerning embroidery machines. There were actually 2 types of embroidery machines, and only recently a third type was developed.

Types of machines

The first type is called "single-head embroidery machine" (see picture 2). This machine has one "head", which means it can embroider one design at a time. In order to start embroidering a second design, the first design must be finished. Of course if the design is much smaller than the hoop, the digitizer can fit multiple copies of the same (or different) design on a piece of fabric, which will be embroidered at once. This, as you understand, is not possible though for designs that are going to be embroidered on a cloth, like a shirt or a hat. The advantage though, is that this kind of machine has more than a one needle; most of them have 10-20 needles, with 15 being the most common number. Having more than one needle is important when one wants to embroider designs with more than one color. With these machines, the color changes are automatic, so it can embroider a 10 color design without stopping at all. Today, most of these machines also have auto-cutting mechanisms. This means that the embroiderer doesn't have to cut small residue threads once the embroidery is finished, like they did in the old times. Now the machine can finish an embroidery design which will be ready to be delivered to the customer with no other intervention.

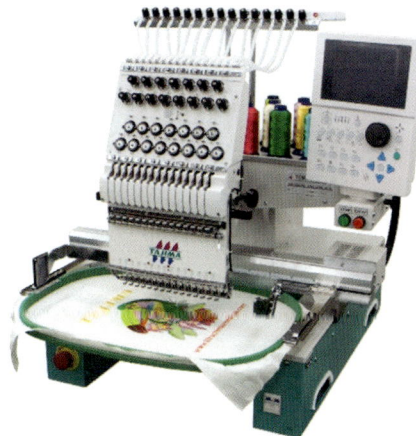

Picture 2 – Tajima Single-head Multi-needle Embroidery Machine

Other characteristics modern single-head machines have are:

- Large color touch screens
- USB interface
- Auto – thread cut
- Changeable hoops
- Built-in basic embroidery editing software
- Embroidery advisor
- Design file storage systems
- Auto tension
- Up to 1300 spm (stitches per minute)
- Laser pointer

Large color touch screens

Large touch screens allow the easy operation of the embroidery machine through the integrated controlling system. A larger screen obviously makes the embroiderer's work easier since he works with bigger buttons, bigger fonts, and is able to see each design picture in a bigger size before embroidering it.

USB interface

All new single-head embroidery machines have USB ports and the ability to read embroidery designs from USB flash drives. This is a very important feature in today's world due to its usability. USB flash drives are part of our everyday life. The ability of embroidery machines to communicate with them was just a predictable outcome.

Auto – thread cut

This is also a very important function you might want to consider before buying an embroidery machine. Auto thread cut means that the machine has a built-in knife, in order to cut thread when is needed, for example before a needle change. Without this ability, a multi-color embroidery design might be a nightmare or even impossible to make, since manual cutting after the embroidery has finished might be too much work or even impossible to do. Almost all modern single-head embroidery machines though have built-in thread auto-cut (knife), since this is a feature that has been in the industry for many years.

Changeable hoops

A hoop is a frame used to keep the fabric taut while embroidering. The embroiderer places the fabric inside the hoop and secures it, ensuring that the fabric is stretched. Then the hoop is secured with special holders attached to the embroidery machine. Most embroidery machines also have changeable hoops. Changeable hoops are another important characteristic you must consider before buying an embroidery machine. Some machines offer more than one hoops along with the machine (maybe 3-4), while others offer just one basic hoop, and sell other hoop sizes as an extra. The third case is that the machine is offered to you in two different prices, one with one hoop and one with full extra, which includes 2-3 more hoops and some other extra accessories. Hoops are not cheap to buy later on, so make sure you get a good deal out of your initial purchase. A new hoop price might start from $100 up.

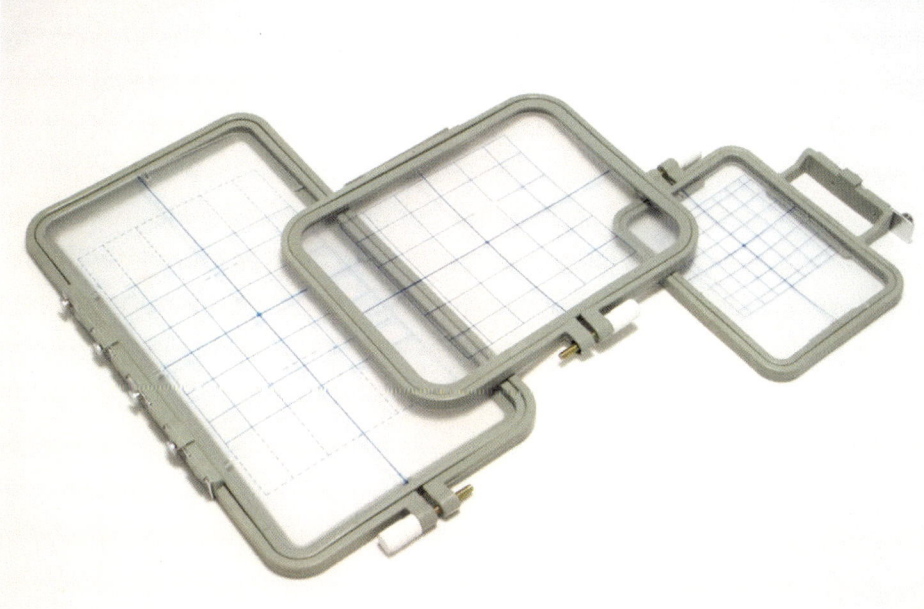

Picture 3 – Different Hoops Sizes

Built in basic embroidery editing software

Many, but not all, modern embroidery machines have built-in editing software. This allows the user to make minor editing to the design before embroidering it. This kind of software of course does not cover the need for embroidery software since it is pretty basic, and is designed only for minor changes. For full editing capabilities plus other functions, like digitizing and monogramming, stand-alone embroidery software is needed.

Embroidery advisor

Some machines have integrated embroidery advisors which are supposed to be offering helpful advice to novice embroiderers. This is clearly a marketing trick, since the advice offered is only basic level, and I would urge you not to consider this an advantage when buying an embroidery machine.

Design file storage systems

This is pretty basic nowadays. In the old days machines only read from floppy disks and had no integrated memory or had a very small memory measured in stitches. For example a machine could hold up to 10 designs with up to 50,000 stitches each. This is not the case any more. Most modern machines have considerable storage size, with easy-to-navigate menus in order to find designs. Just make sure the machine you are about to buy has that feature.

Auto – tension

This is a more recent function in the embroidery machine world. Auto - tension ensures that the tension of the thread is neither too tight-which might lead to thread break, nor too loose-which might lead to poor embroidery result. Normally you can adjust thread tension manually using a knob on the machine, but latest embroidery machines do that for you automatically as well.

Picture 4 – Barudan 20 Head Embroidery Machine

The second machine type is called "multi-head embroidery machine". Multi-head embroidery machines are basically the same as single-head machines multiplied by X. For example a 10 head embroidery machine, can do exactly what a single-head embroidery machine does multiplied by 10. All characteristics and functions are the same as I have analyzed above for single-head machines. The obvious advantage of multi-head machines is that the embroiderer can simultaneously embroider 10 designs, or 20 designs, depending on how many heads the machine has, at the same time. This has obvious advantages on time and productivity for big industries.

This type of machine though is not appropriate for our business model, because of two major drawbacks:

1) It's very expensive. A new multi-head embroidery machine can cost from $30,000 up to several tenths of thousands of dollars.
2) It needs a lot of space. Big industries have big spaces inside their factories and don't face such problems. But believe me, you cannot fit a multi-head machine inside your home. And really you don't have to. Because this is not the business model you should target here. If you want to produce 5,000 pieces of a product, it is pretty sure that a low cost country could do it for substantial less cost, including the shipping to the US or any other western country, due to the difference in salaries and other costs. Remember, this kind of embroidery is dying in the western world. What flourishes is niche market targeting and personalization. That means that your orders will be a few pieces maybe 10-15 maximum. A big portion of your order will be only for 1 piece. The difference is that you will enjoy a much bigger profit margin, which the big industries are not interested in.

So, multi-head machines are something that shouldn't interest you, not now, not in the future of your embroidery business.

The third embroidery machine type is quite recent in the industry. It is basically a sewing machine with an attached embroidery unit, so it is a hybrid of embroidery and sewing machine. It is called single-head single-needle machine.

Picture 5 – Singer Single-head Single-needle Embroidery Machine

These machines can be used as sewing as well as embroidery. There is only one head which is comprised of the needle, thread and bobbin. When a single-needle machine is embroidering, the needle stays stationary, and the embroidery arm moves according to the design that is being digitized. A single-needle embroidery machine only has one point of hoop attachment, and usually has smaller hoop capabilities than a multi - needle machines. Most common hoop sizes are 4" x 4", 5" x 7", 6" x 10" and 8" x 12".

The advantages of this machine type are:

- Price. The most important advantage of this type of machine is its price. You can get it from approximately $600 up to $2,000 depending on the brand and the model. You can even get it cheaper on a promotion day or special deal. This cost is extremely low for starting a business. It allows anyone to start their own embroidery business, and expand to a bigger single-head multi-needle embroidery machine as soon as business expands. If one does only one color monogramming (see BOOK 2), then they might be fully covered with a machine like this, without the need of buying a bigger one.
- Mobility. This machine is very light and small. It is practically a mobile embroidery machine, which you can take with you wherever you go. Most of them even have a practical bag or handle for carrying them. On the other hand single-head multi-needle machines are heavy and big, and are not even close to being mobile.
- You can do sewing work as well. For example if you personalize shirts, and the shirt has a small sewing flaw you can fix it with this machine.
- Most of them are plug-and-play, or have an easy to install software to handle the machine. USB connection is the norm in all brands.
- It is easy to learn how to work with a machine like this, since it is more user friendly than bigger machines.

The disadvantages of this machine type are:

- It only has one needle. That means that if you want to embroider a multi-color design, each time it has a color change you must stop the embroidery process, change the thread, and then resume again. In a design with many color changes, this might be quite time – consuming.
- It doesn't have thread cut. As explained earlier in this book, not having thread cut makes multi-color embroidery very difficult to handle.
- It's not appropriate for multi-color designs.
- It's not appropriate for bigger orders, since it is slower and more fragile than single-head multi-needle machines.
- It has smaller hoops than single-head multi-needle machines.
- It doesn't have hat hoop available, while single-head multi-needle machines do. This is quite important, since a big portion of personalization is expressed through hats, as you already know. The football team of your son, the family reunion or the sales people of a new product, are extremely likely to want to personalize through embroidered hats except of t-shirts, shirts, etc.
- Embroidery speed is usually lower than multi-needle machines, at 300 – 1000 spm, while multi-needle machines usually work from 600 to 1300 spm.
- It cannot perform free arm embroidery, which means that if you want to embroider a pocket, you must rip it off, embroider it and sew it again, while with a single-head multi-needle machine, there are additional hooping systems available, which will allow you to embroider the pocket without the need to rip it off first. Moreover, free arm embroidery makes it possible to embroider bigger embroidery designs.

See comparison Table 1 below, for a detailed comparison of single-head multi-needle embroidery machine and sewing machine with embroidery unit.

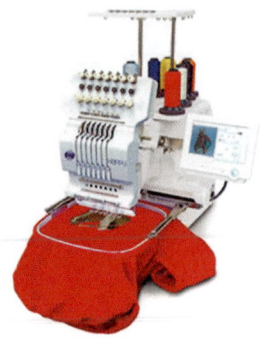 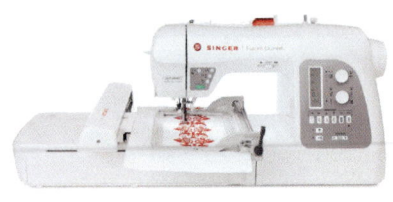

Price $8000 - $15,000	Price $600 - $2000
Not mobile	Mobility
You cannot do sewing work	You can do sewing work as well
More difficult to use	Easy to use-plug & play
It has 5-20 needles	It only has one needle - difficulty in multi color embroidery
Most of them have built-in thread cut mechanism	It doesn't have thread cut - difficulty in handling multi color designs
Faster embroidery speed at 600-1300 stitches per minute	Slower embroidery speed at 300-1000 stitches per minute
More robust	More fragile
Bigger hoops available	Smaller hoops available
Hat hoops available	Hat hoops not available
Can perform free arm embroidery	Cannot perform free arm embroidery

Table 1 - Comparison of Single-needle and Multi-needle Machines

Types of connections with the Computer

The connection of the computer to the embroidery machine is made in order to send the design to the machine. There are other ways to send a design to the machine without directly connecting it to a computer. We will review all possible ways now.

- ✓ If you decide to buy an older embroidery machine (it will be multi-needle, since in the past there was no embroidery unit for sewing machines) it is possible that it will have an attached floppy disk reader, which was quite common in the past. The problem is that modern computers do not have floppy drives any more, and to tell you the truth it is obsolete. So, if you are about to buy an embroidery machine which has floppy drive for reading designs, make sure there is another input method possible. Many of those older machines can receive USB reader device which is sold as an extra from the manufacturing company. You can ask them about the cost of this device in order to calculate your investment. The price should be around $800 for this device. Quite expensive if you ask me.
- ✓ All older machines also have parallel or serial input port. The older ones have parallel and most recent ones serial port. Your computer must have parallel or serial port as well in order for you to be able to connect the machine to the computer via cable. Parallel is obsolete and no computer has parallel ports any more. You might find a serial port in a second hand computer, but you can also use a serial to USB converter. So, if you want to buy a second hand single-head multi-needle embroidery machine, a serial connection might be fine with you. The serial connection is not the usual 9 pin that you may know of, but a 25 pin connection, referred to as "DB 25" (see picture 6).

Picture 6 – DB 25 Serial Cable

- ✓ USB input port or USB cable is a must in latest embroidery machines, single and multi-needle ones. In the case the machine has USB input port, you must save the embroidery design in a USB flash drive and then connect the flash drive on the machine. The machine reads the design from the USB flash drive, and then it is ready to embroider it. In the case of USB cable, you must connect one side of the cable to the computer and the other side to the embroidery machine. Most likely, the embroidery machine will have some kind of embroidery software accompanying it,

which will allow you to send the embroidery design to the machine through the cable.
- ✓ LAN. Some machines support LAN connection which allows sending the design through a LAN cable.
- ✓ Most modern embroidery machines also have integrated Wi-Fi connection protocols, which allow the transmission of a design from the computer wirelessly. The computer or tablet must also support wireless connection protocols, and will probably need software provided by the embroidery machine manufacturer, in order to communicate with the embroidery machine. More and more embroidery machine manufacturers add Wi-Fi connection capability to their machines. The future trend as I see it will be transmission with Wi-Fi from tablets or smartphones, using specialized applications sold by the embroidery developers or the embroidery machine manufacturers.

Machines for home based business

Since we have seen all available embroidery machine types, it would be very useful to examine which one is more appropriate for home based embroidery businesses.

As you can see in Chart 2, the answer to this question is connected to two different variables: projected monthly production, and available investment funds.

If your projected monthly production is approximately up to 150 embroidery artworks per month and/or your budget for buying a machine is up to $1,000, then a single-head single-needle machine is the one appropriate for you. If you are planning on doing more embroidery products per month, up to maybe 500 or a little more, and your budget can stand around $10,000 then a single-head multi-needle machine is appropriate for you. For a bigger production scale, a multi-head machine is needed, raising the investment cost to about $40.000 for a production of 5.000 products per month.

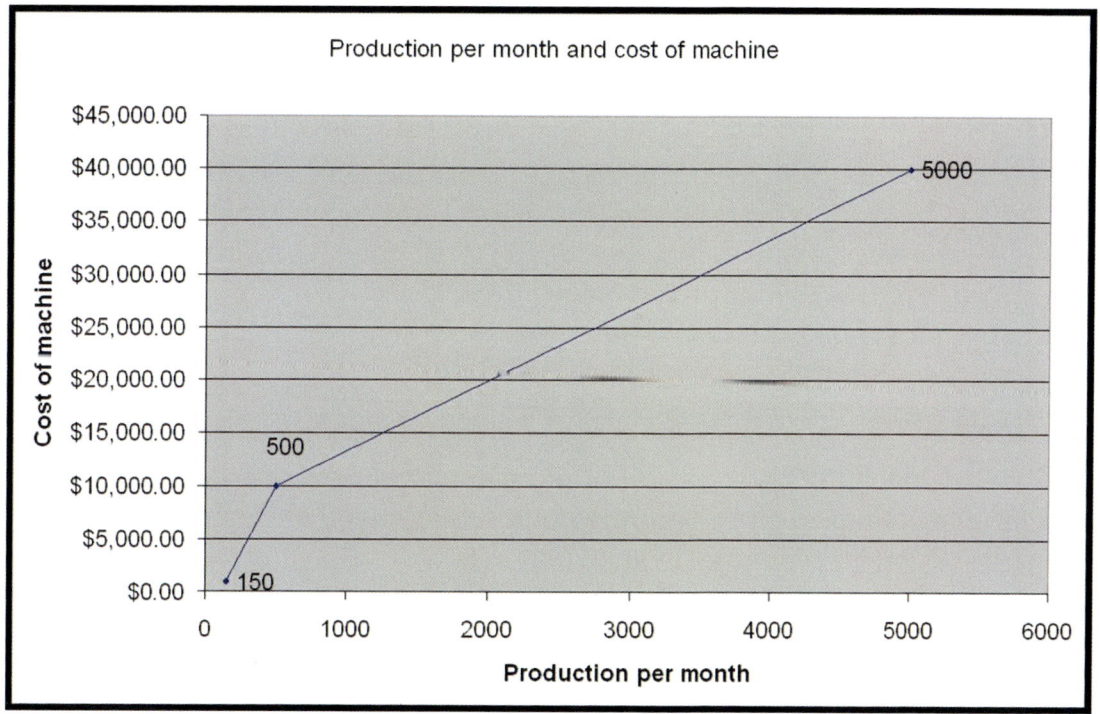

Chart 2 – Production per Month and Cost of Embroidery Machine

The above analysis is a bit simplified and takes into account only 2 factors, projected production and available funds. There are other factors that might lead you in one or another purchase. For example, even if you have low production per month, let's say 80, but your niche market obliges you to create big sized embroidery designs with many colors, this factor alone will lead you to a single-head multi-needle purchase, despite having low production per month. The difference is that if you sell in a niche market like this, the profit per product will be much higher, so your total income per month will justify the investment in a single-head multi-needle embroidery machine. Later on I will present more exceptions from this rule.

Generally, single-needle machines are appropriate for starters, for many reasons. First of all you need to determine if this work is good for you, if you like it and if you are happy with it. If you are not, you can always leave it back. Investing big from the start is not a good idea, if you don't have any previous experience in embroidery, or if you are not sure you can do this at least for some time until you reach the Break-even point of your investment.

Secondly, a single-needle machine is always useful, even if you buy a multi-needle machine in the future, for the following reasons: a) you can keep it as backup for times that your multi-needle will have a problem that will stall your production for a day or two. b) you can take it with you wherever you go, in order to keep working everywhere, and c) even if you don't need it any more, you can always sell it. The money you have invested on it will not be wasted; on the contrary it will be well spent.

Thirdly and most importantly, single-needle machines might actually be all that you will ever need, depending on your niche market! For example, if you only do one color monogramming on t-shirts, you don't actually need a bigger machine, if your work is limited and you want to keep it this way due to limited time from your end (e.g. if this is your second job and not your primary).

The conclusion is that single-head single-needle embroidery machines are always very useful to modern embroidery professionals involved in niche market sales.

Single-head multi-needle embroidery machines though, are the next step for all of you that will start the embroidery business from home professionally, or have previous experience or your targeted niche market requires one. This is the basic and most important tool in your hands, a robust professional machine, with capability to offer substantial quantity production units, in reasonable time. This machine type can lift you up to a different world. I promised that I will make you a state of the art digitizer and I will, but without this type of machine, your artwork cannot reach at the 100% of its potential. Multi-needle embroidery machines are the core of this industry, and for the most of you it will be the roof of industrial machinery that you will need to buy, since as I already mentioned, our purpose here is not to produce thousands of products per month with lowest price possible, but make smart money out of niche markets.

So, buy a single-head multi-needle embroidery machine, only if you are sure that you are going to stay in this profession, or if you have previous experience in it. Of course resale value for this type of machine is quite good, but I would suggest you follow my advice on this. With a machine like this, you are fully covered for all niche markets that you might decide to chase from home. If your work rises exponentially, you can always buy a second single-head multi-needle machine to match rising demand, or... raise the price if you don't want to dedicate more work time...but I will tell you all these marketing secrets along the way.

Exceptions from the rule of production – cost as shown in Chart 2 would be the following:

- Type of embroidery as mentioned above. Even if you have fewer than 150 pieces per month to produce, but these are big embroideries with many colors each, multi-needle machines are a one-way road for you. Also, if you have more than 150 pieces per month, but these are tiny one-color embroidery designs, you can keep your single-needle machine until the point that the machine itself cannot stand the production.
- If mobility is an important factor for you, single-needle is the machine for you. If you also need to create big embroideries with many colors, then you might need to buy both machine types.
- If you need to do embroidery on caps or embroideries big in size, then single-needle machine cannot serve you; multi-needle machine is for you, even if production is less than 150 pieces per month.
- If you need to do sewing as well, then single-needle machine might be a good choice instead of buying a sewing machine, because of all the advantages discussed above, of course as long as your budget can handle this.
- Of course it all depends on your budget, so if for example your budget can only buy you a single-needle machine, but your niche market demands a multi-needle machine, then I would suggest you find another niche market, until you raise the capital needed to invest in a multi-needle machine. You never know, maybe the other niche market that you will choose fulfills your expectations and you never need to move forward, it's all up to you!

So, all in all, the best embroidery machine for home embroidery business is actually the one that best fits your needs. Since now you know the differences between the embroidery machine types, and you also have guidance on how to make your decision, move on and don't be afraid, enter the magic world of embroidery now! Next, I will give you detailed information on machine brands.

List of machine brands

Back in the seventies things were pretty simple; there were very few manufacturers of embroidery machines, and the prices were hitting the sky. Nowadays there are more than 2000 embroidery machine manufacturers, producing more than 50.000 machines per year, when in the late seventies production was approximately 2000 machines per year. Of course even today, quality machine brands are not more than 10, with all the other being cheap Chinese and Taiwanese machines. I will list here the top of the industry, and I would advise you to stick on one of those brands, and if your budget is lower than their price, go for a second hand embroidery machine instead of going for a no name Chinese one. More or less all below brands have similar prices of around $8,000 - $15,000 for a single-head multi-needle machine, so I will focus in other quality info on each brand without repeating the price each time. Firstly I will present the brands which mostly sell single-head multi-needle machines, then the ones who sell both, and lastly the ones which only sell single-head single-needle machines.

TAJIMA

Tajima is a Japan based embroidery machine manufacturer with offices in the USA and China, and 42 agents in various countries. It offers single and multi-head multi-needle embroidery machines. It does not offer single-head single-needle machines. It has an established cooperation with embroidery software developer "Pulse" (see Chapter 3), and offers embroidery software called "Tajima DG/ML", which is of high quality, with some minor problems and failings.

Tajima is one of the most popular brands nowadays. It produces high quality machines, with normal price. In the past it had much better prices in order to compete with "Barudan" which was the market leader. Now that Tajima is established as quality manufacturer, prices rose to normal levels, or even considered expensive some times.

Customers are generally happy with Tajima quality of machine and quality of embroidery artwork.

Website: http://www.tajima.com/

BARUDAN

 Barudan is also a Japan based embroidery machine manufacturer with offices in UK, Canada, USA, Brazil and other places around the world, and 95 agents to many countries of the world. It has an established cooperation with Compucon (see Chapter 3) embroidery software developer, who has develop software TES for Barudan, and with Wilcom embroidery software developer. Both above software are of high quality, with Wilcom being the leader of the embroidery software market.

Barudan used to be the leader of the embroidery machine market in the past, but now, as many of as see, lost this place from Tajima. Nonetheless, Barudan remains one the biggest embroidery machine manufacturers, selling high quality machines. Barudan also has one of the most developed and efficient support network in the industry. Customers are generally happy with Barudan machines and after sales service, as well as with embroidery artwork quality.

Website: http://www.barudan.com/

BROTHER

Brother is also a Japan based embroidery machine manufacturer with a huge distribution network including offices in many places of the world like the USA, UK, China, South Africa etc and 66 agents around the world. Except from embroidery machines it sells a lot of other products, for example printers, and has also developed its own embroidery software called "PE Design". PE Design though has stopped being developed, so it is not advised to buy it.

The last 3 years, Brother has pulled out the professional embroidery machine market, and now only sells machines for the home market and small professionals, which is mainly single-head single-needle and single-head multi-needle machines with specialization to low needle number machines, that is 6 or 8 needles.

Brother also has a huge selling and support network around the world, with excellent marketing departments. Quality is high, but the advertizing part of the cost in each machine is higher than the other two above brands. Customers are generally happy with Brother and its support network, but old customers would say that quality is lowered in comparison with past years, but still remains in relatively high levels.

Website: http://www.brother.com/index.htm

HAPPY

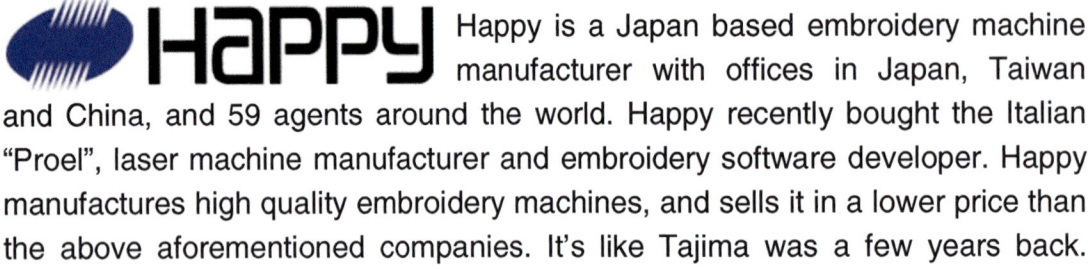

Happy is a Japan based embroidery machine manufacturer with offices in Japan, Taiwan and China, and 59 agents around the world. Happy recently bought the Italian "Proel", laser machine manufacturer and embroidery software developer. Happy manufactures high quality embroidery machines, and sells it in a lower price than the above aforementioned companies. It's like Tajima was a few years back.

After sales support is of high standard, but in any case bit lower than the previous 3 giants. Customers are generally happy with…Happy, and that is why this company gains market share every year.

Website: http://www.happy-ind.co.jp/product/embroidery.html

MELCO

Melco is another Japan based embroidery machine manufacturer with offices also in the USA and 156 agents around the world. Its present in the US is very strong, and they make a lot of effort on this. Their machines are of high quality, but a bit lower than above mentioned manufacturers. They sell software called "Design shop" along with their machines, which is mediocre quality software.

Customers are generally happy with their machines, but there are complaints about after sales services. More specifically, support in older products of the company is non existent as many customers complaint. This is important, because an investment on an embroidery machine is going to be for many years, so one would expect high quality support for at least 10 years.

Website: http://www.melco.com/

ZSK

ZSK is a Germany based embroidery machine manufacturer, also having offices in the USA and another 97 agents around the world. It manufactures high quality embroidery machines, which are being accompanied by software called "EPWin" and "BasePac 8". They try to provide good after sales service, but their strong point I would say is the machine quality. In recent years they do not follow technology gadgets on machines and their marketing budget is substantially lower of that of other competitors, but their machine quality stays high. Generally people are happy with their machines, but not with their software.

Website: http://www.zsk.de/

RICOMA

Ricoma is a China based embroidery machine manufacturer with strong presence in the USA and 25 agents around the world. It is one of the "quality" Chinese machines, almost comparable to the previous Japanese ones. It also sells "D.I.S.C." embroidery software, which is of mediocre quality.

Customers seem to complain on electrical problems in Ricoma machines, while the mechanical part of them seems to be working just fine.

Website: http://www.ricoma.cn/

SINGER

I believe everyone knows Singer, since it is one of the oldest companies in the sewing machine market. I bet very few of you know that Singer bankrupted in 2004, and was sold to an investment fund. Also, Singer today belongs to a company group called "SVP", initials of the first letters of the companies that participate in this trust, that is Singer (American) – (Husqvarna) Viking (Swedish) – Pfaff (German). All three companies are manufacturers of sewing machines and, in recent years, single-head single-needle embroidery machines. Singer machines are not of the quality they used to be when your grandmother bought one, but they have adapted to what the new economy demands, that is lower cost and lower lifetime for all products. Compared to competition though, SVP still produces quality machines, which to tell you the truth though, incorporates a relatively high marketing cost percentage in their price… That is, it is a bit more expensive because they are called

"Singer", and because Singer has more marketing expenses than a smaller company.

After sales service is of high quality, and available in almost all countries of the developed and developing world. There are a lot of complaints from customers for the quality of smaller and cheaper sewing machines from SVP, but at least for the single-head single-needle embroidery machines, feedback is better, since quality is much better as the price goes up. "Singer Futura" is the name of their single-head single-needle embroidery machine, and they offer "Futura" software with it, which is developed by "Compucon" embroidery software developer. Huqsvarna and Pfaff have their own single-head single-needle embroidery machines, which are of similar quality.

Website: http://www.singer.com/

JANOME

Janome is a Japan based sewing machine manufacturer with offices in many countries like USA, Canada, UK etc and 63 agents around the world. They offer high quality sewing machines, and single-head single-needle embroidery machines. They also offer software "Digitizer Pro" developed from "Wilcom" embroidery software developer.

Customers are generally happy with Janome machines, since they keep high production standards. They also sell OEM machines, so you might find the same machine under some other brand name, at a lower price. A good example is the German "W6-Wertarbeit" which sells Janome machines in the German market through the internet at a lower price.

Website: http://janome.com/

So, based on the analytical presentation of embroidery machines in previous pages, we can sum up the following. You can choose a single-head multi-needle machine between the following brands:

- Tajima
- Barudan
- Brother
- Happy
- Melco
- Zsk
- Ricoma

You can choose single-head single-needle machine between the following brands:

- Brother
- Singer
- Janome

As I mentioned earlier, I would not advise you to buy a cheap Chinese or other low cost country produced machine, since it will most likely create many problems, have difficulty reading embroidery design file formats, produce low quality embroidery, and most importantly will not have after sales support. One of the most known Chinese embroidery machines is called "Feiya" and is promoted a lot. It has higher quality that other Chinese machines, but again cannot match the top brands. If you don't have the budget for the above mentioned machines, just go for a second hand machine. Now that you have the list and all the inside info for most of them, you can choose wisely based on your needs and budget.

How to choose the best machine for you

I have already explained in detail how to choose the best machine for your needs, and also have provided all the tools and knowledge that you will need in order to do this. So, just let me sum them all up here.

There is no "best machine" for everyone; there is "the best machine" for each one of us. So, the best machine is actually what will cover your needs in the most efficient way with the smallest cost, in order to bring the higher possible income to you. So, as mentioned earlier it is all connected to your needs and your budget. Your alternatives would be single-head single-needle or single-head multi-needle machine, or both. What you want to exclude from your options, at least for the start, is multi-needle machine. Chapter 4, which explains the business model of home based embroidery business, will help you choose your niche market and also calculate the total investment needed for you to start, so this will determine the kind of machine(s) you will need, at least for the start. Earlier in this Chapter, you were presented of all the available embroidery machines, comparison tables, connection types and all available big brands, so with all this knowledge, plus the path that you will follow after reading Chapter 4 and finishing this course in general, will help you decide which embroidery machine you will purchase. This course is designed to help you choose what is best for you. I bet you were blind, as far as embroidery is concerned, but now you are half blind, you know the types of the machines, differences between them, connections, brands etc. If it wasn't for this course you would acquire this info after many years of research and experience. Well, I promise you, that when you finish this course, you will know exactly what to do and how to do it. You will be able to start making money from the very next day, so keep on and stay positive.

Outsourcing embroidery

One last option you might want to consider, at least for the start is outsourcing embroidery. Most of the embroiderers until now were actually outsourcing digitizing and were doing embroidery themselves. Of course digitizing is much more difficult. In the new age though, I would suggest you consider outsourcing embroidery, and do the digitizing yourself, at least for the start. Many people would think I am crazy, but these are the same people that are closing down their businesses and actually outsource to low producing countries. I ask you to consider outsourcing in your local market. I will explain why you can do that successfully right after.

The secret here is that you don't want to produce mass products with as low cost as possible in order to gain profit from the number of units sold. Low cost producing countries are doing this nowadays and you just can't compete with them. You want to produce high quality unique products that the customer will be willing to pay much more for. Many times you might have noticed that embroidery quality in clothes is poor. This is not acceptable for your business. You will offer standard or high quality fabric, with top quality embroidery. What you are actually selling in a niche market, is not a t-shirt with embroidery, but embroidery on a t-shirt. I don't know if you get the difference. The customer doesn't buy the t-shirt because of its quality, color, brand etc. He buys it for the personalized embroidery. If the t-shirt you sell is of good quality that's just an advantage for him/her, not the feature that will determine his/her decision on whether to buy it or not. The customer will buy your products because of the quality and the uniqueness of the embroidery.

So, as you understand, your main work here is the embroidery digitizing not the actual embroidery or the quality of the fabric. Of course all factors determine your end product, but the weight each one has in your customer's decision is different. The extra cost to create high quality product, is well spent, since it will get back to you multiplied by your satisfied customers.

So, outsourcing embroidery is a possibility that you might want to consider, at least for the start, or maybe for your business model in general. While making up your mind, you can consider the following points:

- ✓ Outsourcing embroidery will reduce the initial investment a lot, since the embroidery machine is one of the most expensive parts of your business. Moreover, by outsourcing, you can focus on niche markets that would have required a multi-needle machine, which you might didn't have the funds to buy. So, an obstacle is removed from your path. Someone would say that the cost would be bigger, and the profit for you smaller. Well read my next point and decide for yourself. Also, have in mind, that the price that you will get from a professional embroiderer if you give them the embroidery design, will be much much lower compared to asking him to digitize the design for you as well.

- ✓ By outsourcing embroidery, you will have more time to focus on digitizing, which will make you an even better digitizer, and on marketing and organizing your business. In the end, this will potentially bring you more income, since the more quality work you deliver (embroidery digitizing) plus the better marketing you do for your products, the better your turnover and subsequently your earnings would be. So, don't be short sighted, you will have a lot of things to do at the start, and the more time you have for the important things that bring immediate money, the better results you are going to have.
- ✓ Embroidery digitizing is difficult to learn, but the actual embroidery with the machine is tricky also, especially in big and multi-colored designs. It will take you some time in order to learn how to perfectly embroider a product, but outsourcing embroidery, will allow you to have high quality products from day one of your business. You might even consider outsourcing embroidery the first few months of your business even if you buy a machine, until you master the art of embroidery yourself. Remember, quality, and most importantly the embroidery quality is number one factor of decision for your customers.
- ✓ If you focus in two different niche markets, or if you have different types of design difficulty in the market, you can also consider buying a single-head single-needle embroidery machine, in order to cover demand for what you can with that type of machine, and outsource only designs that cannot or are very difficult to be done with that machine type. This will allow you to also deliver multiple orders in shorter time, since 2 machines (yours and your embroiderer's) will work at the same time in order to cover your orders.
- ✓ It is most profitable to focus on Embroidery digitizing, since you can sell your experience separately and at a quite high price. You can offer embroidery digitizing services to others (even to your embroiderer) and earn a substantial amount of money from it, since few offer embroidery digitizing services, and even fewer are really good on it. A good digitizer can earn a lot of money out of digitizing for others. A plus for this is that you can sell this service over the internet to a vast customer worldwide base. Sure, there is a lot of competition on the internet, but believe me, most of it is junk low cost low quality digitizers. Quality digitizers are very

few even on the internet. So, focusing on this along with the main focus on embroidery could bring some substantial extra income to you.

The most important thing to keep in mind though concerning outsourcing embroidery is that you need to find a good professional, not too far from your home, which can offer normal prices for any quantity. All of the above 3 conditions must be met:

1) The embroidery professional will be your partner. In order to start your business you want to minimize factors that would possibly affect your work, so finding a good partner is vital. You don't want him to stall your orders, or to put your orders behind of others of his customer's orders. You don't want him to raise the prices without earlier notice, or give you low quality embroidery because he is too tired. You can even buy fabrics and threads yourself, to minimize quality loss in case the embroiderer wants to minimize cost and uses low quality threads or fabrics. You need to discuss all these from the beginning, and let him know that this is the start of a long cooperation, if both parts are ok with their obligations to each other.

2) Your partner mustn't be too far away, because you might pay him a visit even everyday. Your type of work will be such, that you will be required to deliver orders each and every day, with many of them being low unit orders, that is 1 or 2 pieces. So, as you understand, if your embroiderer is far, this distance will add a substantial cost to your end products, which sometimes might be unbearable, if for example one day you have only 1 or 2 orders, and the fuel in order to get to the embroiderer's place and back is too much. Not to mention, that he might not be available when you get there, and you might be needed to drop the design and possibly the fabrics and threads off, and collect it at a later time. So, distance between you and your embroiderer is also a vital element of your business when outsourcing embroidery.

3) Prices are always negotiable, but if you live in a smaller town and there isn't much competition there, the embroiderer might request high prices. It's up to you to calculate your costs and your buying prices, but negotiating embroidery pricing if you decide to outsource is also vital. If you are not happy with the prices you got, ask elsewhere, or negotiate

further. Do whatever you need to do in order to get normal prices. You don't want to drop quality for lower cost, so request normal price for top quality, not low price for low quality.

If you have problem in finding a good embroiderer near you, then buying an embroidery machine might be a one way road for you. A last thing you might want to consider, is finding a good embroiderer who fulfils the 2 of the 3 elements we discussed above, except the distance. You can send him the embroidery digitized file with an email, and he can embroider according to your instructions. Then the product can be sent to the customer from his site, and not come to you first and then to the customer, because this might result in high shipping for you. Higher level of trust is needed here though, since you will not be able to check the end product before dispatching it to the customer, plus you must trust that the embroiderer will always be there when you send the shipping company to pickup the products in order to deliver to the end customer.

Embroidery outsourcing has its pros and its cons, and again it depends on your specific needs and planning, to decide if this might be a feasible solution for you or not. Nonetheless, if you don't think embroidery outsourcing will work for you, just remember that it's an alternative that you have, and you can keep it in the back of your mind in case you ever consider using it.

Chapter 3 – Embroidery Digitizing

Now that you are into the embroidery world, and that you have learned about embroidery machines, let me proceed to the important parts of modern western world embroidery, which is "Embroidery Digitizing".

What is Embroidery Digitizing

As I already mentioned, embroidery digitizing is the process of converting artwork into digital data, which is then used to get it stitched onto a piece of fabric or other material through a computerized embroidery machine.

Embroidery digitizing is the most important part of the embroidery business, since if the embroidery is badly digitized there is nothing you can do in order to counterbalance this flaw with careful embroidery on the embroidery machine. So, the actual design must be perfect, and good embroidery outcome starts with a perfect design.

I have already explained the value of embroidery digitizing, and how expensive it is to hire a skilled embroidery digitizer, in order to produce high quality embroidery files for you. So, digitizing yourself is the key for the success of your business, since your will save all this money that you would pay to a digitizer, plus you will be able to sell your digitizing services to others, which will bring substantial extra income to you, plus you will be able to control the quality of the designs and change them accordingly.

In order to do all the above though, you will need two things:

1) You will have to be a good digitizer and
2) You will have to purchase the tool that will allow you to create embroidery designs, i.e. the embroidery software.

About point 1, I will help you become a good digitizer by teaching you all the things you need to learn in BOOK 2 of this course, plus all the little secrets embroidery digitizers use today. Concerning point 2, we will examine it in this Chapter.

Buying embroidery software is not an easy thing to do, and surely it's not cheap. So, choosing the best embroidery software for your needs is vital. Most embroidery software developers offer one professional and one semi-professional software. The alternative to that strategy would be to have basic software and offer function add-ons, depending on each customer's needs, which some developers indeed do.

As in the embroidery machine market, there are many industry secrets in the embroidery software market as well, that I will of course share with you as I promised. I will give you all the inside info, which software is good and which just has good marketing, plus I will give you approximate prices for most software. You need to know though that sometime prices differ a lot from one country to another in embroidery software. I have often observed such huge price differences, which is just difficult to explain and even weird. I suppose this is called bad business and poor planning. Anyway, let's move on and see the biggest embroidery software developers in the world, and learn secret inside info about their products.

List of embroidery software developers

Wilcom is one of the oldest embroidery software developers with headquarters in Sydney, Australia and offices in USA, UK and China. They also have a huge distribution network of 147 agents around the world. It is considered to be the market leader of embroidery software today. Its owner gone bankrupt in 2013 which was a big hit, and now the company is under external administration. They have managed to keep their market leader position though. Their software is a bit complicated but produces high quality stitch result, which is the most important thing to consider.

Wilcom updates its software frequently and most times provides high quality support. The users are generally happy with Wilcom, except for some complaints about their support department, difficulties on switching from Art Canvas to Corel Draw X6 in their newest version, plus complaints about the prices, which indeed are high. Wilcom has two kinds of embroidery software, one professional and one semi – professional. The professional one is called "Embroidery studio" with 3 levels E1 – E3, and price at around $8,000 - $15,000 depending on the level and on the market you are buying it from. This price is indeed very high for the modern market. The secret here is that Wilcom does substantial discounts if you ask them to do so. So, pretend you have a better offer, or that you simply can't afford it and that you are going for another developer. They will surely offer you a better price.

The semi – professional software offered from Wilcom is called "Deco Studio" with levels E1 – E3. Prices here go from $1,000 - $3,000. Again you can get substantial discount if you play it right.

Wilcom is the embroidery software supplier for Ricoma, Janome and Barudan, and also cooperates with Corel, which is in a way incorporated into their software.

Website: http://www.wilcom.com/

Pulse is another big embroidery software developer, with its headquarters in Canada and 69 agents around the world. Pulse has strategic partnership with Tajima embroidery machine manufacturer. It also cooperates with Elna and has cooperated in the past with Toyota.

They develop and sell "Tajima DG/ML" embroidery software, through Tajima. The software price varies from $2,200 to $5,000, depending on the level (it has 4 levels) and on the market.

Users are generally happy with the software, except for some "bugs" that haven't been fixed yet, like a color display problem, complaints that the software hangs up frequently etc. There are also many complaints about their online tech support, and their complicated website policy, since they have too many websites for no reason, and the average user is confused when he wants to contact them or find online support. The software though produces high quality stitches, which is why Tajima chose to sell it along with their machines.

Website: http://www.pulsemicro.com/

Compucon is an embroidery software developer with headquarters in Greece and offices in the USA and Japan. It also has 49 agents across the world. Compucon is considered to be the former market leader before Wilcom. The last years though it has lost in efficiency and marketing, which resulted in losing substantial market share.

Compucon is cooperating and develops "Futura" software for Singer, which accompanies Futura single-head single-needle machines, plus develops "TES" software for Barudan. Also, it develops and sells its own software called "EOS" and "Stitch & Sew". EOS is the professional software, with prices from $900 to $6,200, and Stitch & Sew the semi – professional with prices from $600 to $2000 depending on the level and the market.

In general, users are satisfied with Compucon software, after sales service and quality of stitches produced, but are complaining for bugs in both of its software. Moreover Compucon hasn't issued a new version for its software for many years now. It only supports them with critical updates. The end user price after some negotiation is substantially lower than that of Wilcom, even Pulse, and the software is of high quality and easy to use, but the buyer doesn't know if the company will continue to support their software and issue new versions in the future. This is very important, since an investment in embroidery software is not negligible, and one would expect full support for many years after the initial purchase.

Website: http://www.compucon.gr/

Sierra is a US based embroidery software developer with 14 agents around the world. They offer 2 different software levels of "Stitch ERA", their software. One level is for professionals, with cost of $2,200 and one for starters with cost of $1,400. They also offer their web based software in $ per month lease, which might be a good solution for someone who doesn't want to invest much in embroidery software from the start. There are many complaints for their web based (leased) version of the software though, and most claim that it is not comparable to the normal version, which I verify. Their web based software is limited, has lots of problems, and their tech support is not good. On the other hand $10 or $15 a month is not so much, as one could argue. Remember, you are going to sell embroidery designs on fabric, not fabric with embroidery design, so this part of the job is not the one to cut expenses from. If you choose Sierra I would advise you to go for the full version.

Their software is quite simple and easy to use, but with limited functionality. There are many complaints for their tech support and after sales service. Their stitch quality is descent and will do the work at least for your initial steps.

Website: http://www.freesierrasoftware.com/

Wings is another embroidery software developer with Headquarters in Greece and 18 agents around the world. They are a more recently established company than the above and surely smaller in numbers. They develop descent embroidery software, with mediocre stitch quality. Their software though has a lower price range than the rest of the companies mentioned above, and many customers buy it for this particular reason.

Wings develops and sells 2 different types of software: "Drawings 6 Pro" is their professional software, and its price varies from $1,250 to $1,650 depending on the level and the market. "Drawings 6" is their semi – pro software with prices varying from $310 to $750. The customers are generally happy with Wings, but there are some complaints about stitch quality and capabilities of their software. Their after sales service is good, but their market share is quite small.

Website: http://www.wingssystems.com/

The companies mentioned above are the biggest and most important software developers in the world. I would suggest you stick on the first three or at least on these five. In order for you to get the full picture though, I will mention some smaller developers that might interest some of you:

- Floriani based in the USA
- Embird based in Slovakia
- Embrilliance based in the USA
- Buzz tools based in the USA
- Generations based in the USA
- Icliqq based in UAE
- AllCAD Technologies based in Hong Kong
- CadCam technology based in the UK
- Sew good based in the USA
- Proel based in Italy

How to choose the best embroidery software for you

Choosing embroidery software -and level accordingly- is not an easy thing to do, and surely isn't cheap. On the other hand, embroidery software is your basic tool for this job, so choosing the right one for your needs and keeping it within your budget limits is very important.

As you understood I support choosing software from one of the bigger companies, since this will offer you quality of stitch, ease of use and after sales support, which is quite important. Time is money in this profession as well as in others, so wasting time with problems is not acceptable. By choosing software from one of the smaller companies (as I have also mentioned about Chinese embroidery machines), you might face problems related to the quality of the stitching, the actual digitizing process, or general stability of the software. All of them will result in big problems. Quality of stitching is the worst problem you might face, since customers will not be forgiving for this. Remember, you sell embroidery <u>on</u> fabric, not fabric <u>with</u> embroidery, that's a different market! For example, when one might pay $30, $50 or $100 in order to get specific embroidery design on a t-shirt, and they get crappy embroidery, it is certain that they will not buy again from you, plus they will probably discredit you to many other people. More specifically, researches have shown that one disappointed customer will discredit you to an average of 20 other people in his personal life, so do the math for 500 or 1000 disappointed customers. Also you need to consider internet discrediting, since those 20 people mentioned above come from his personal circle of family and friends! An internet comment could be viewed by several thousands.

If the digitizing process of the software is very complicated it will cost you in hours of working. Time is money, and you can use all these extra hours of work to promote your products, or sell your digitizing services to others, so easy-to-use software is important to you. Of course I am referring to the comparison of quality between same types of software (professional-professional or starter-starter software comparison), since professional software cannot be as easy to use as starter software. Some level of complication cannot be avoided, in order to offer a higher level of functionality, which is desirable, since once you learn to use the software well, this higher functionality will help you digitize a lot faster, thus sparing you time. Starter software are much easier to learn, but when it comes to complicated designs, it will take you twice the time to digitize a design because they don't have the tools that professional software have to make the process easier and faster.

If the software has general stability problems, it means that it might hang up while you are working, or shut down abruptly. This might create big problems to you, since you might loose hours of work if you haven't saved it, or even get frustrated and don't be able to continue the digitizing after multiple shut downs. Other stability problems might be low speed, problems in handling big embroidery files with many thousands of stitches, etc.

People say "you get what you paid for" and this is also true for embroidery software. So, if you want top stitch quality you should get software from one the first three or five companies I mentioned. Wilcom is the leader but ridiculously expensive due to high marketing costs, plus it is a bit more complicated than it should be according to what it offers. Pulse software, is similar to Wilcom, but with lower prices and less advertising, since it mainly sells through Tajima embroidery machines. Compucon software is also good as the above and even cheaper than both of them, but they haven't issued a new version for many years now. Their support though is very good, and they keep their software up to date by issuing compatibility and bug fix updates. Sierra and Wings are of slightly lower stitch quality than the above three, but still within professional levels, so they are also an option to you. As you can see none of the above companies is perfect, and none is the obvious choice to make. That is why I am giving you all inside info, and you can choose for yourself. The only advise I give you is stick to big companies for your embroidery software and don't try to cut off costs from this purchase.

I bet things are a lot clearer now, but still you are a bit confused on what to choose. So let's try to make it even clearer for you. First of all, you need to decide if you are going to buy new or second hand software, depending on your budget. If you are going to buy second hand you really need to look for what is offered on the market, since the alternatives will be limited to this. If you are going to buy new, there are more options. For new software, you need to determine if the work you need to do can be done with starter level software, or if you need a professional one. In general, letters, simple logos and monograms can be created with starter software as long as the specific software level has digitizing, monogramming and editing functionalities. So, if for example you are just doing monogramming on shirts, starter level software will be fine for you. You will even be able to digitize simple logos and other simple designs. When I say simple I don't necessarily mean one color or ridiculously simple like two circles and a rectangle! You can easily digitize logos like Ford's or Google's:

Picture 7 – Logos to digitize with starter software

If you need to digitize logos more complicated than the above or want to have more functions available, like for example "color blending" (see BOOK 2), you will have to go for professional level software. With professional level software you will be able to digitize almost all kinds of images, letters, even photos. It will be more difficult to learn and get accustomed to, but once you do, you will be able to finish a job much faster, since the tools you will have at your disposal will make your work easier. Also, you will have some tools available that will allow you to digitize many images that starter software won't allow you to. So, if your niche market requests simple designs, you can invest on a semi – professional (starter) embroidery software, but if you want to offer more complicated work to your customers, or if you want to sell your quality digitizing services, professional digitizing software is more appropriate for you. Consider your embroidery software as your tool or as an asset for your work, because that is what it is. So, choose it wisely and invest appropriately in it.

Embroidery files

In embroidery digitizing every machine can read ("understand") different file types, so embroidery software developers have incorporated those file-types into their software. Most software today can export designs in all file-types that big brand machines can read. Apart from that though, all embroidery software have an internal file type that is unique for every brand. For example, Wilcom is using ".emb" files, Pulse ".pxf" files and Compucon ".erf" or ".che" files depending on the software. These file-types are called "block files" and are different than the ones the machines read, which are called "stitch files".

If you digitize a circle, you and your embroidery software might see a circle but the embroidery machine only sees a bunch of stitches, it does not have the capability to group it in a circle form, and "understand" that this is a circle. So, when you save you design in an internal embroidery software format, like .emb, .pxf or .erf then this is saved in linear form, which is fully editable for future edits. On the other hand stitch files, which are what all the file-types that embroidery machines can read are, are not saved in linear form. They are only consisted of a group of stitches, which is not fully editable in the future. Software developers have created tools that allow people to edit stitch files as if they were block files, but this type of editing results in a certain loss in quality, and it is not advised to do so. So, what you need to do once you buy embroidery software and start working with it, is save all your files in both formats, most importantly as block files, in order for them to be available for future editing and also in stitch format for embroidering it or delivering to the customer if you act only as digitizer. Thus you will have each design in two different files a block and a stitch file.

Below you will find an extremely useful board. It contains most embroidery software and embroidery machine file types alphabetically, and you will not find such detailed information anywhere else:

Embroidery machine/software alphabetically	File type/Extension
Artista	(.ART) vector format
Babylock	(.PEC, .PEL, .PES) Note: PES comes in Types 1, 2, 2.5, 3, and 4.0
Barudan Beat 900	(.DC2, .DD2, .DM2, .DP2, DS2)
Barudan FDR "U code" (1.4 MB)	(.T03, .U01) The 2 digits after U are the pattern number
Barudan M7000	(.DAT)
Barudan	(.EXY, .FXY, .UXY)
Bernina	(.PEL, .PES) Note: PES comes in Types 1, 2, 2.5, 3

	and 4.0
Brother	(.PEC, PEL, .PES, .PHC) Note: PES comes in Types 1, 2, 2.5, 3 and 4.0
Crosstitch	(.KRZ)
Data-Stitch	(.STX) vector format
Melco	(.EDS)
Elna	(.SEW)
Elna Xquisite	(.EMD)
Embird	(.STX) Vector format
EOS by Compucon Ver. 1 & 2	(.REF is the native vector, .XXX)
EOS by Compucon Ver. 3	(.ERF is the native vector, .REF is v.2 native vector, .XXX)
ES-65 by Wilcom	(ESL, .T01, .T03, .TO4, .TO5, .EMB is vector format)
Gunold	(.PCH, .STC)
Happy	(.TAP)
Huamei	(.DST, .DSB, .DSZ)
Husqvarna & Viking	(.CSD, .HUS)
Inbro	(.DST)
Janome	(.JEF, .SEW)
Kenmore	(.SEW)
Melco	(.CND is vector format, .EXP)
Microstitch	(.STN)
Mitsubishi	(.10o)
OESD Simon, Jr. from Oklahoma	(.OEF)
Origins	(.ASD, .DST, .EXP, .HUS, .PES)
PE-Design 5 by Brother	(.DST, .EXP, .HUS, .PEM, .PES)
Pfaff	(.KSM, .PCS home, .SEW)
Pfaff	Macintosh (.PCM)
Plauen	(.t10)
Proel DOS	(.PUM)

Proel	(.ARC, .PMU)
Prodigy	(.PCD & .PCQ)
Punto by SofTeam	(.PDC)
Richpeace	(.DSB, .DST, .ZSK)
Saurer	(.PAT, T15)
Shiffli	(.ESL)
Singer	(.XXX)
Singer EU	(.CSD, .PSW)
Tajima	(.DST, .DSB, .DSZ, .T01)
Tajima DG/ML by Pulse Microsystems	(.KWK, .PED, .PSF)
Tajima DG/ML by Pulse Microsystems	Version 10 & up (.PXF)
TES from Barudan (EOS clone)	(.ERF is native vector format, .XXX)
Toyota	(.10o)
Viking Designer 1	(.SHV)
Zangs	(.T04)
ZSK	(T05, .DOS, .DSZ)

Table 2 – Embroidery File-types

Martin Barnes [EMBROIDERY BUSINESS FROM HOME]

Chapter 4 – The business model of home based embroidery

In the previous chapters we have learned basic things about embroidery, shared information on modern embroidery, embroidery machines and embroidery software and much more. Now embroidery must seem much simpler to you, and you must be starting making business plans of your own. Well let me help you and make it very simple for you.

In Chapter 1 – "Basic things to know about embroidery", we examined the embroidery industry size and its potentials, we analyzed various business related subjects, like what you need to invest in followed by estimated costs and explained how one can make a living out of embroidery. In this Chapter I will present a complete business model for home based embroidery, with all important details you will need in order to start your own embroidery business from home.

Where to start from

So, where does someone start in order to make an embroidery business from home? The first two things you need to determine are whether you can work from home and if your home is suitable to work from.

Working from home is becoming the new American dream for many people, but it's not for everyone. It is a thought that would make many people happy but ultimately some of them could not manage it. Even if working from home could make them a fortune, they wouldn't be able to do it. You must be wondering why, so let's see the advantages and disadvantages of working from home:

Advantages:

- Flexibility

- Proximity to home and family
- More time with children
- Less stress
- Less distractions
- More productivity
- Better work/life balance
- Better health
- Reduction in travel time
- Saving some expenses like office rent, telephone and other expenses shared between house and work

Disadvantages:

- Difficulty in separating work from home
- Isolation
- Domestic distractions and interruptions
- Need for self – discipline
- Work doesn't end
- Lack of human interaction

As you can see there are some pros and cons in working from home. If you ask me the advantages surely overcome the disadvantages, but there may be some people that really can't stand isolation for example or domestic distraction is too much for them. Well if you are one of them you can just try to work it out, for example insulate a room of your home if it is too noisy. For the vast majority of you that don't have second thoughts, let's proceed to number 2, i.e. if your home allows you to work from it.

This is pretty simple. You just need to determine if you have all required things to work from home. Just consider if the following are available to you:

- A room at least 250-300 square feet in order to fit a single-head multi-needle machine and a desk with a computer, or smaller if you are going to use a single-head single-needle machine. The room floor should be

hard and strong in order to hold the embroidery machine's weight when it embroiders for long hours
- Internet access which will allow you to handle your internet sales, your website, your emails and advertising campaigns
- A telephone connection in order to assist customers through telephone and possibly raise your sales
- A computer with Wi-Fi, USB and sufficient RAM memory (at least 4GB), sufficient hard drive space (at least 500GB), and large screen in order to be able to digitize easily. The screen should be at least 17 inches, and ideally it would be 22 or 24 inches. Also, a mouse and a keyboard.

After making sure you are good to go as far as the previous two prerequisites are concerned, the next thing is to choose your niche market.

Niche market

A niche market is a subset of the market that a specific product is focused on. For example sport TV or documentary channels are a niche market of TV in general. What one has to do is to focus all marketing efforts on a small but specific and well-defined segment of the population, by identifying and satisfying needs, wants and requirements that are being addressed poorly or not at all by other firms, and developing and delivering goods and services to satisfy them. The strategy in this is that it is better to be a big fish in a small pond rather a small fish in a big pond, and, believe me, this strategy is very profitable.

How -you may ask yourself- can I compete with existing competitors that already have experience and are bigger than me? Well, that's all about niche marketing. You must find a micro market that is not well satisfied, or you must satisfy a need in a micro market better than the existing competition. Remember, the price is not so important in micro markets, since people are willing to pay more. Competition from bigger firms is non existent, since it is simply not profitable for them to satisfy those needs. Big firms buy/produce in huge quantities in order to get better prices, and they try to buy/produce products that will satisfy as many consumers as possible. This leaves a huge market outside of their reach, and they will never try to reach those customers, because they simply don't care since it is not profitable for them to care about 100 or 50 or even 1 customer.

Well, you will, and those customers will be willing to pay much more for your services or products, because they will not find them anywhere else, or because they will not find this quality anywhere else. That is why I won't stop reminding you about offering top quality.

Those niche markets are real gold mines for small entrepreneurs that are truly professionals, offering top quality products and first class services. So, what you need to find out is your niche market. It could be personalized gothic embroidery on hats or Church embroidery on scarves, Hawaiian embroidery on pāreu's or just personalized monogramming on shirts. Whatever your niche market is just be a professional and let the public know you are a professional. Sell them an integrated product that includes fabric, embroidery and after sales services, not just a shirt.

If you can't choose a niche market, just start by offering personalized embroidery on various types of cloth or whatever else a customer might want, and in the future your niche will come to you.

Overview of the business model

Your website

The embroidery from home business has great potential on the internet, which will be your main area of business. What you need to do is create or pay a professional to create a website for you. Your website must depict your niche market everywhere and most importantly on the landing page. A landing page is the page of your website that a user is "landing" when he presses your domain address directly or when he finds your website from search engines, such as Google. So, your landing page must be very carefully created in order to show your customers that:

- ✓ You are doing personalized embroidery
- ✓ You are doing embroidery for a specific niche market
- ✓ You are a professional
- ✓ You are probably the only one or the best one in this specific niche market

- ✓ You sell worldwide
- ✓ You don't have any hidden costs
- ✓ You offer after sales services
- ✓ Their purchase is guaranteed
- ✓ Their payment is done in a safe way

I would advise you to focus on the quality of your work rather than price offers. Most people interested in niche markets are willing to pay more as long as the quality of the product is very high. So, advertise excellent quality and offer excellent quality, never trick a customer; this is the secret to becoming rich. It might sound simple enough, but you will be astonished on how many professionals start with these values and on the road they just forget them and change their way of doing business. I advise you not to change. Every single one of your customers is precious and must be treated this way, even if he made the smallest order. Remember that this customer will order again in the future, and will also advertise you to his friends in the same niche market. From my experience when a customer is pleased he tells it to an average of 6-7 others, but when he isn't he tells it to 18-20. Multiply that with the internet potentials in forums etc, and there you have some tens of thousands! So, every customer is gold.

Apart from your landing page, you can also present your previous work, and also some designs that the customer can choose from and personalize them, by adding their name for example. So, a presentation of your portfolio is another important thing to have in your website. Just keep in mind that since you offer personalized products, you cannot offer online payment to your customers without prior contact with you, except if you offer some standard products in a mini e-shop inside your website, like designs for a specific niche market on shirts, blouses, etc, which a customer might choose from. This will require more work from the website creator and a higher cost, but will result in better business for you, since online customers that are interested in something tend to search a lot and thus the more content you have in your website the better.

Another thing you can present to your website is that you are really a master in your niche market, so add content like articles with advises and ideas for your customers, for example "How to wash a shirt with embroidery on it and not spoil it".

As for your digitizing services, I would advise not to offer them in the same website, since it will make you look unprofessional by trying to earn more money from side – work. Just create a second website to offer those services, or offer them elsewhere on the internet, or even talk to local embroiderers. My opinion is that doing all these three together is most efficient. Just make sure that the website you are going to offer embroidery digitizing services to, is professionally made, presenting an impressive portfolio with very high quality designs. You must be the master who can do something that few others in the world can. Do this successfully and trust me, once you make your name, people will pay a lot for your services. That of course premises that you are able to deliver high quality embroidery designs.

How the business works

Once you have everything set up, it's time to start working. The way this business model works is as follows: You advertise yourself on the internet (see next sub chapter for more details) and drive traffic to your website. If you have an e-shop you will have orders to deliver every day you open your emails. If you don't, then the customers will contact you through contact form, email, telephone or any other form of communication you might offer (like Skype), in order to put orders or ask details about them. Once you agree on an order and a price, or once you have an order from the e-shop, you must create and deliver it. So, if the order requires you to create a design with embroidery software you must create it and then embroider it on whatever cloth you agreed with the customer (e.g. on a t-shirt). If it is an order from the e-shop it might not require you to digitize anything if the design is from your catalog, or it might require you to just add something to an existing design (like just adding a person's name). Once you embroider it you must pack and send it to the customer.

But what about payment, one might ask. Well, you can offer various payment types, all in advance of course. An e-shop must have online automatic credit card and PayPal payment options, so be sure to add this feature or request your website designer to do so. For customers that will contact you first to ask for info or negotiate, and don't want to pay automatically through the e-shop, you must offer at least credit card, bank transfer and PayPal payment options. Some professionals already started accepting payments in digital coins as well, for example bitcoin. That is something that distinguishes them from competitors and might attract a niche market, which can be customers who have bitcoins to spend and want to buy personalized embroidery products. I bet no – one else in the world offers this yet. For those of you who are not familiar with bitcoin, it is a digital coin which can be transformed to US dollars anytime you want. For more info you can visit https://bitcoin.org/en/.

Where to advertise

You can always offer you products locally, thus advertise yourself in local newspapers, TV stations, radio, etc, but most of your work will come from the internet, were you will have millions of potential customers. Once you determine your niche market, you must start an internet advertising campaign. First of all you need to find the group of people you are trying to reach, their interests, age, gender, etc and also you need to find appropriate keywords related to your business. Keywords are what people type in Google or other search engines, in order to find what they are searching. So, you need to ask yourself what a person will type in Google in order to find personalized Hawaiian embroidery for example. Some alternatives might be:

- ✓ Personalized Hawaiian embroidery
- ✓ Hawaiian pāreu with embroidery
- ✓ Hawaiian pareo with embroidery
- ✓ Embroidery on Hawaiian pāreu
- ✓ Embroidery on Hawaiian pareo
- ✓ Hawaiian embroidery
- ✓ Hawaii embroidery pareo
- ✓ Hawaii embroidery pāreu
- ✓ Best Hawaiian embroidery
- ✓ Quality Hawaiian embroidery

And so on, you get the picture. Whatever a person might think to write in order to look for what you offer is a potential keyword for you. You must wonder why keywords are so important for you. Keywords are what you use when you advertise in Google. The basic concept is that you tell Google: "whenever a person searches for this keyword, show my advertisement and I will pay you X amount of dollars". Depending on how much money you give to Google, it will show your advertisement to more or less people. Moreover, the cost is not fixed but it depends on how many competitors use the specific keywords to advertise as well. So keywords like "Hawaiian embroidery" will cost much more than "Embroidery on Hawaiian pāreu" since they are being used by more people and thus more advertisers target them. Thus Google will more likely ask you to pay close to $1 per click for the first and maybe $0.15 per click for the second. You can choose to pay less than Google asks, but then Google will show your advertisement very few times, only when there is no higher bidder for this keyword. So, advertizing in Google its bidding for the keyword and Google show the advertisement of the highest bidder, since this is how they make more money! I would advise you to target as many keywords as possible within your target niche market, and pay a little bit more in advertising, at least during your first steps, until you have created your customer base.

So, where to advertise on the internet? There are a lot of places to do so:

- ✓ Google
- ✓ Facebook
- ✓ Banner advertising campaigns in websites frequented by your target market
- ✓ Develop links from as many websites, directories, meta – indexes frequented by your target market as possible
- ✓ Develop a feature product on the first page of your website every week in order to keep customer returning to your website frequently
- ✓ Creating a mailing list and send free e-zine (electronic magazine) or newsletters to customer's emails and advertise new products in it
- ✓ Provide updates via RSS
- ✓ Join an affiliate network
- ✓ Register in all major search engines
- ✓ Agree a linking arrangement with non-competitive website
- ✓ Create YouTube channel and show your products and your expertise in videos that you will upload

✓ Create Facebook and Twitter pages, where your customers can learn the latest news from you

Below you can find a short explanation on how each of the above works. For more info, you can buy an internet advertising book or course to learn more. Explaining more in this course is out of its purpose:

Google: Google is the worlds largest advertising alternative for internet advertising. It shows advertisements in its search engine and in Google Adwords partners, which consist of thousands of websites around the world. Google shows your advertisement only in people who search similar things in its search engine, and also in partner websites that are similar to your product. Advertising in Google is highly efficient and can boost your work and profit. I would advise you to definitely include this in your planning.

Facebook: Facebook is one of the most successful social networks of our time, used by millions of people around the world. It offers extremely targeted advertising, and you can focus your advertising through many variables like gender, marital status, country, language, age and many more attributes of your target market.

Banner advertising campaign in websites frequented by your target market: You can contact website owners of websites that have content that interests your target market, and request them to add a banner advertisement of your business to their website. They will inform you of the daily, weekly or monthly cost you must pay.

Develop links from as many websites, directories, meta – indexes frequented by your target market as possible: This is a free form of advertising in most cases, since most of those websites, directories and meta – indexes offer basic entry for free and only charge for extra features. It is very important that the customers can find your firm in all catalogs, and it is also very important to create as many links as possible to your website as well.

Develop a feature product on the first page of your website every week in order to keep customers returning to your website frequently: Also, do whatever else you think could bring a customer back to your website frequently, since more frequent visits could bring more frequent orders and more income for you. This is also for free.

Creating a mailing list and send free e-zine (electronic magazine) or newsletters to customer's emails and advertise new products in it: It is very important to keep in touch with your customers, so keep their emails at all cost. Once you have created a mailing list, send them newsletters or your e-zine frequently in order to keep in touch and to advertise your products for free.

Provide updates via RSS: RSS stands for "Rich site summary" and in a few words it means that you provide frequent updates and news which the customer reads instantly using the appropriate RSS reader software. It is also a good free way of advertising and keeping in touch.

Join an affiliate network: This is also a must do. Affiliate networks are pages on the internet where product creators like you create products and offer them, and the affiliates choose to sell them for a commission. An affiliate is like an agent of yours who sells your products for a commission. The more the affiliates who sell your products the more sales you will have. Joining an affiliate network might change your life. What you need to consider though is that the level of personalization here is limited, since the affiliates must know the price before they sell, so prices are fixed. What you can sell with the help of affiliates is embroidered clothes (or whatever other embroidered material) with standard designs of your niche market, and maybe offer personalization by adding the customer's name or something similar. Further level of personalization might require a higher price which is not possible since the customer will have already paid when you receive the order.

There is also a second benefit for you here. Not only the affiliates will boost your sales by bringing customers to you, but they will also create a loyal customer base for you, which will most likely return for further purchases, since that is how niche market customers behave. Plus, when they buy from you again, you will have a better profit margin, since the affiliate will not be an intermediate any more.

Register in all major search engines: This is obvious and free of charge. The more search engines index and thus show your website in relevant search terms, the more traffic your website will have, resulting in more orders and income for you.

Agree a linking arrangement with non-competitive websites: Linking arrangement means: "I will advertise you in my website and in return you will advertise me in your website". It is that simple. Both parts are favored since they are not competitors, but they have the same customer base. An example for the

Hawaiian pareo business would be a website selling sunscreen products, since most customers will want the pareo for their summer holidays.

Create a YouTube channel and show your products and your expertise in videos that you will upload: This is a very effective and free advertising option. YouTube is very popular and many businesses already advertise their products there for free by uploading content videos. Let your imagination roll and create fancy professional videos which will show your quality products and expertise through short videos. Also, be sure to upload other content videos like "How to preserve an embroidered pareo for 20 years" stuff. Your customers will appreciate such videos a lot, plus you will look even more professional to them.

Create Facebook and Twitter pages, where your customers can learn all the latest news from you: This is also simple and free. Just make sure you tweet and write Facebook posts frequently. If you are not going to do that, then just don't bother creating such pages altogether. A non-updated Twitter or Facebook page is worse than a non-existent one.

If you think all these are very hard for you, there are companies that specialize in internet marketing and will help you on this. This will add another cost for you, but without internet advertising you simply cannot work from home, except if you have a lot of local deals, but this is different than the business model proposed in this course. Do not hesitate to contact me if you need help in your internet advertising planning. I will happily help you achieve your goals and your dreams.

Additional Income

Except for your main business, you can offer some additional services in order to make some extra money from your embroidery business:

- ✓ Offer your digitizing services
- ✓ Offer special personalized packs for weddings, christenings, wedding or baby showers and other special events
- ✓ Offer several levels of gift wrapping
- ✓ Sell banner advertising to your website(s) for non-competitive companies

Believe it or not, I know people who make the same or even more money from additional services like these than from the main embroidery service or products that they sell.

Initial Investment Analysis

I am pretty sure you are excited with all these valuable info I offer you, but let's examine the initial investment one must make in order to start an embroidery business from home. In Table 2 below, you can see initial investment calculations for two different business types. One is for single-head multi-needle embroidery machine and professional software, plus all the other things you need to invest in the beginning, and the second is for single-head single-needle embroidery machine and starter software plus all other things needed.

Let me state that you can start an embroidery business from home with any one of those two alternatives. In chapters 2 and 3, we have examined the advantages and disadvantages of each machine and software type, so it is really up to you to decide which one of the two business types below is appropriate for you. If you want to start slowly, maybe as a part time job at first, and invest as little as possible until you learn the work, you must choose the second alternative model. If, on the other hand, you want to fully commit yourself and be a professional from day one, or if you have previous experience in embroidery and internet marketing, you can choose the first alternative model. Whatever you choose, if you really commit yourself and produce high quality products, find the correct niche market and do the right advertising, then you will see what I mean when I say that the smart ones can really make money of personalized embroidery today. So, let's see what you need to initially invest, and explain each one:

Asset	Estimated Cost in US dollars
Single-head multi-needle embroidery machine	$11.000
Initial machine consumables	$400
Initial fabrics supply (shirts, t-shirts etc)	$1.500
Professional embroidery software	$5.000

Desktop computer	$700
Website(s) creation services	$3.000
Various expenses (legal paper work etc)	$1.000
Total Initial Investment	**$22.600**
Single-head single-needle embroidery machine	$1.500
Initial machine consumables	$200
Initial fabrics supply (shirts, t-shirts etc)	$1.500
Starters Embroidery software	$1.000
Desktop computer	$700
Website(s) creation services	$3.000
Various expenses (legal paper work etc)	$1.000
Total Initial Investment	**$8.900**

Table 3 – Initial Investment required

As you can see, an indicative cost for the first case is US $22.600 and for the second US $8.900. These figures are absolutely realistic and will not be far from what you will actually need to invest in if you choose rationally. Let's see what you need to invest in:

- ✓ Single-head multi-needle or single-needle embroidery machine. You can find all appropriate info in Chapter 2.
- ✓ Embroidery digitizing software. You can find all appropriate info in Chapter 3.
- ✓ Initial machine consumables. This includes all consumables related to the embroidery machine like threads, needles, glue, etc.
- ✓ Initial fabrics supply. Depending on what products you are going to offer, you must buy initial supplies. These are the cloth or whatever else that you are going to embroider on. That supplies might be "blank" shirts, t-shirts, jackets, hats, socks, etc
- ✓ Desktop/laptop computer. A computer with Wi-Fi, USB and sufficient RAM memory (at least 4GB), sufficient hard drive space (at least 500GB), and large screen in order to be able to digitize easily. The screen should be at

least 17 inches, and ideally it would be 22 or 24 inches. Also a mouse and a keyboard.
- ✓ Website(s) creation services. Fee for the website designer, plus all the costs involved in this like buying a domain name for your website(s), hosting services, maintenance for a year, etc. If you can do this by yourself, you can exclude most of this cost, and keep only what you actually will pay, like hosting services.
- ✓ Various expenses. These include anything that might be associated with establishing your firm, like expenses for paperwork which may vary depending on which country or US state you are residing. Those expenses also include costs for a new telephone and internet connection, if you don't already have one in your house.

Sum up

At this point let's sum up the steps you need to follow in order to create your home-based embroidery business:

1. Make sure you can work from home
2. Make sure your home is appropriate to work from
3. Find you niche market(s)
4. Do an internet research about your niche market(s)
5. Establish your firm and make all appropriate paperwork
6. Buy your equipment and familiarize yourself with it
7. Create your website(s)
8. Plan your advertising strategy and start implementing it immediately
9. Think of additional income services and incorporate them in your business
10. Allow at least one year until you see the first positive results except if you are experienced in embroidery and internet marketing. In that case the first positive results should be expected in as soon as 3 months.

Follow the above steps, exploit the knowledge you got from this book, and proceed with confidence in creating and expanding your embroidery business from your home. Don't just read this book only once like it being a novel, but consult it whenever you have a question or you are in a cross road about the next steps of your early embroidery career. In the next and final volume of this course (also available at Amazon) I will teach you all the embroidery digitizing secrets the embroidery digitizers don't want you to know, plus techniques on how to calculate cost and selling price of your products.

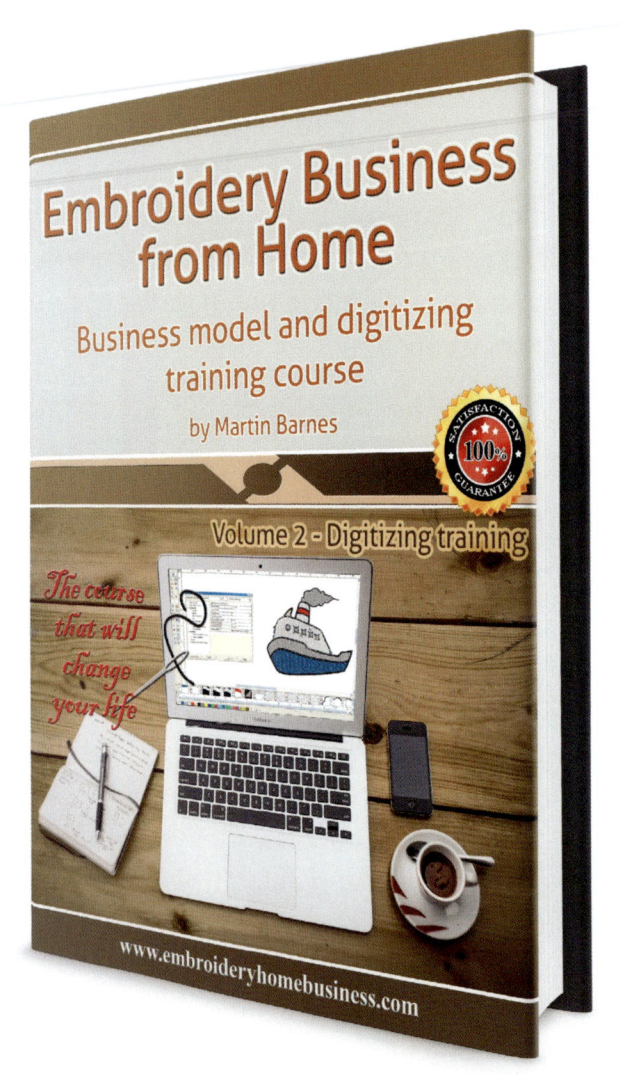

For a complete knowledge, it is advisable to also watch the 3.5 hours HD training videos that accompany this book. You can buy it at a special price along with 40 high quality embroidery designs from www.embroideryhomebusiness.com/extras. This offer is only available for Amazon readers, so you need to input the exact internet address as you see it above. You will not find this offer page if you visit the Home page of my website EmbroideryHomeBusiness.com.

How to get the Free Embroidery Designs

If you truly liked this book, and you would like to share this opinion with others by posting a review to the store you bought this book from, we will be happy to compensate you for your time and your confidence to us by sending you 5 ready to be stitched embroidery designs for free. For example, if you bought the book from Amazon.com, the procedure would be the following:

1. Go to the store that you bought the book from, e.g. Amazon.com, and post a 5 star positive review on this book. Sincerely write the reasons you liked the book, and how it helped you. The comment must come from a verified purchase. For example, if you have purchased the book from Amazon, and you write the review using the same account, the purchase will automatically be verified.
2. Go to www.embroideryhomebusiness.com, click contact, complete the required fields, and in subject field write "I am interested in the 5 free embroidery designs from Volume 1" (if you decide to buy volume 2 there is a similar offer with different 5 designs)
3. In the comments of the contact page write "My name is Martin Barnes (replace with your name) and "I have bought the Embroidery business from home volume 1 from Amazon.com". My Amazon.com nickname is "Martin.Barnes" (replace with the name that is visible when you comment and post reviews on the store that you bought the book from) and I have just commented positively on your Book at website www.amazon.com. Please send me my free embroidery designs".
4. After verifying your review, we will email you the 5 embroidery designs, and written permission to embroider them even for commercial use. Make sure to check your spam folder as well in case your email provider falsely lists our email address as spam.

Please note that in no case we want you to post a positive review if you did not like my book. In that case, I urge you to contact me and explain why you did not like the book. I carefully listen to my readers in order to improve future editions of my books.

Printed in Poland
by Amazon Fulfillment
Poland Sp. z o.o., Wrocław